CANADA'S COASTAL ANIMALS

Chelsea Donaldson

Scholastic Canada Ltd.

Toronto New York London Auckland Sydney
Mexico City New Delhi Hong Kong Buenos Aires

Every reasonable effort has been made to trace the ownership of copyright material used in the text. The publisher would be pleased to know of any errors or omissions.

Visual Credits

Front cover, pp. i, ii (borders), iv–1, 3, 5: © Thomas Kitchin & Victoria Hurst; pp. i (centre), 22: © Roberta Olenick/Never-Spook-the-Animals Wildlife Photography; p. iv: © HotHouse Design Studio; p. 2: © Index Stock/Maxx Images; pp. 4, 8–9, 27, 28: © Tom & Pat Leeson; pp. 6, 44 (bottom): U.S. Fish & Wildlife Service; p. 7: © Robert Maier/Animals Animals–Earth Scenes/Maxx Images; p. 10: © David Wrobel/Visuals Unlimited; p. 12 (top): Norbert Wu/Minden Pictures; p. 12 (bottom): © Richard L. Carlton/Photo Researchers/First Light; pp. 14, 16, 17: © Fred Bavendam/Minden Pictures; p. 18 (top): © Ralph Reinhold/Maxx Images; p. 18 (bottom): © Rosalie V. Borzik; pp. 19, 24: © age fotostock/Maxx Images; p. 20: © IFA-Bilderteam/Maxx Images; p. 21: © Frank Todd/Arcticphoto.com; p. 25: © blickwinkel/Alamy; pp. 26, 34: © SuperStock/Maxx Images; p. 29: © Steven Kazlowski/Leeson Photo; p. 30: (top) © Lynn Stone/Animals Animals–Earth Scenes/Maxx Images, (bottom) © A.B. Thomas/Animals Animals–Earth Scenes/Maxx Images; p. 31: © M. Baird/Ivy Images; p. 32: © Mark Bowie/Animals Animals–Earth Scenes/Maxx Images; p. 33: © Ronald Wittek/age fotostock/Maxx Images; pp. 35, 36–37: © Ron Niebrugge/Accent Alaska; p. 38: © David Hoffmann/Accent Alaska; p. 40: © James Watt/Animals Animals–Earth Scenes/Maxx Images; p. 41: © Doug Perrine/Pacific Stock/Maxx Images; p. 42–43: © Michael S. Nolan/age fotostock/Maxx Images; p. 44 (top & centre): National Oceanic and Atmospheric Administration/Dept. of Commerce; back cover: © Mark Mandic

Developed and Produced by Focus Strategic Communications Inc.
Project Management and Editorial: Adrianna Edwards
Design and Layout: Lisa Platt
Photo Research: Elizabeth Kelly

Special thanks to Dr. Bill Freedman of Dalhousie University for his expertise.

Library and Archives Canada Cataloguing in Publication
Donaldson, Chelsea, 1959-
Canada's coastal animals / Chelsea Donaldson.
(Canada close up)
ISBN 978-0-545-99736-2

1. Coastal animals—Canada—Juvenile literature. 2. Marine animals—Canada—Juvenile literature.
I. Title. II. Series: Canada close up (Toronto, Ont.)
QL122.2.D645 2007   j591.77'0971   C2007-902224-3
ISBN 10: 0-545-99736-4

6 5 4 3   Printed in Canada 119   12 13 14 15

MIX
Paper from
responsible sources
FSC® C103113

TABLE OF CONTENTS

Welcome to the Coasts!   **1**

CHAPTER 1: **Starfish**   **2**

CHAPTER 2: **Pacific Salmon**   **5**

CHAPTER 3: **Eel**   **10**

CHAPTER 4: **Octopus**   **15**

CHAPTER 5: **Atlantic Puffin**   **18**

CHAPTER 6: **Great Cormorant**   **23**

CHAPTER 7: **Sea Otter**   **26**

CHAPTER 8: **Sea Lion**   **30**

CHAPTER 9: **Dall's Porpoise**   **35**

CHAPTER 10: **Humpback Whale**   **39**

Canada's Coasts

- North Pole
- Arctic Ocean
- Alaska
- Pacific Ocean
- Canada
- Atlantic Ocean
- United States

- Canada's Coasts
- Canada
- United States

Welcome to the Coasts!

A coast is an area where the ocean meets the land. Canada has the longest coastline in the world. We have the Pacific coast in the west, the Atlantic coast in the east and the Arctic coast in the north.

The animals that live along our coasts have found different ways to live there. Many spend all their time in the water. A few can move easily between land and sea, while others can live in both fresh and salty water. Those with wings can fly over the water and dive beneath it.

Let's meet some of these amazing animals!

CHAPTER ONE

Starfish

Starfish are odd-looking animals. They have no ears, no nose, no legs, no front or back . . . and no real brain. That's right, no brain! While that would be a problem for us, starfish have managed to survive this way for millions of years.

In place of a brain, starfish "think" with their arms, which are called rays. Scientists are not sure exactly how this works. Their best guess is that if one arm senses food, it can take charge and tell the other arms to move toward it!

On the underside of each arm are hundreds of sensors that look like tiny tubes. These help starfish move around and hold onto things. They also have suction cups for climbing up smooth surfaces.

A starfish may not have a brain, but it has a mouth. It's on the underside of its body, right in the middle. A starfish's favourite snacks are mussels, clams and oysters. A starfish can push its whole stomach out of its mouth. The stomach wraps around the starfish's prey and . . . GULP!

Starfish come in many sizes, shapes and colours. The smallest are about the size of your baby fingernail, and the largest are almost as big across as both your arms stretched out.

Most starfish have five rays, but some kinds have as few as four or as many as twenty-four. Starfish can be pink, purple, yellow or many other colours.

If a starfish loses one of its arms, it can grow a new one. Some kinds of starfish can even grow a whole other starfish just from one arm. That's really amazing for an animal with no brain!

CHAPTER TWO

Pacific Salmon

Pacific salmon spend most of their lives in the salty ocean. But before they die, they finish a journey that started when they were born.

Salmon are born in freshwater rivers and streams. Then they travel to the ocean. Some of them will swim up to 1200 kilometres to get there! Years later, the salmon travel all the way back to the place they began.

But the salmon have changed along the way. Each stage of its life has a different name.

Salmon begin their lives in the fall as pink, see-through eggs that are buried in gravel at the bottom of a stream. Soon, a pair of eyes looks out from each egg. A few months later, the eggs hatch. Small fish with bright orange sacs attached to their bellies swim out. These odd-looking babies are called *alevins* (AL-uh-vins). They stay hidden in the gravel, away from predators.

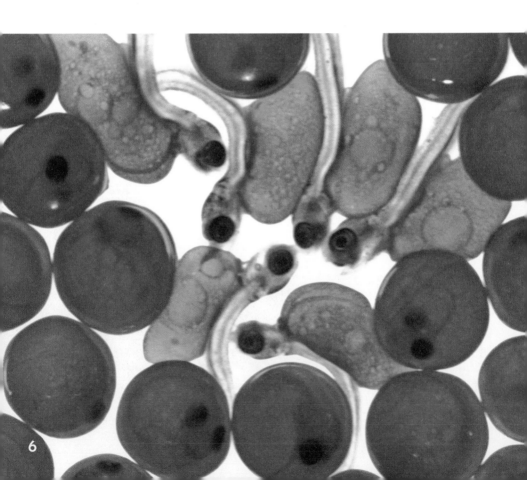

By May or June, the orange sacs have disappeared. The young salmon then enter the stream as tiny fish, called fry. Some may live in lakes for up to a year, while others head for the ocean right away.

When a fry reaches the ocean, it spends the next three to five years eating and growing. Then one summer day, the adult salmon begins its amazing journey back to the same stream where it was born. No one is sure exactly how it finds its way.

This time, the trip is even harder because salmon have to swim upstream against the water's current. They often have to leap up rapids and waterfalls in their way. It's exhausting! Also, salmon stop eating when they leave the ocean, so they are starving by the end of their journey.

When a salmon finally arrives at its birthplace, it spawns: a female lays hundreds of eggs, and a male fertilizes them. Soon after, both the male and the female die. But the eggs they left behind soon turn into tiny alevins . . . and the cycle begins again.

CHAPTER THREE

Eel

They're slimy. They're slippery. They look like underwater snakes. They hide by day and come out in the dark to feed. On stormy, moonless fall nights, thousands of them begin a mysterious journey to the hidden depths of the ocean.

No wonder some people find eels a little creepy! But eels are amazing fish. Their "creepy" habits have helped them survive for millions of years.

Like salmon, eels travel long distances to and from the sea. But they do it in the opposite direction from the salmon. Eels begin their lives at sea and head for the coast.

In the fall, some adult eels swim out to sea and never come back. About six months later, young eels start to arrive along the east coast. For a long time, no one knew where the adult eels went or where the young ones came from.

Scientists now think that adult eels spawn in the Sargasso Sea, which is a part of the mid-Atlantic. Eels lay their eggs so deep under the water that no one has ever seen them. Scientists believe that the adult eels die once the eggs are fertilized.

At first, baby eels,
or larvae, look like
long transparent leaves
with eyes. As they grow,
they drift with the current
toward the coast. They begin to
look more like adult eels. At this stage,
the young eels are called elvers.

Some elvers spend their lives at the
mouths of rivers where the water is partly
salty and partly fresh. Others move inland
to live in freshwater rivers and streams.

Eels don't turn into males or females until they reach a certain length. Those that live in crowded areas where food is scarce are likely to be male. In larger rivers, like the St. Lawrence, where there is lots of food, almost all the eels become females. Female eels are much larger than the males.

Once they settle, eels usually stay in one place for up to 20 years. (One eel in Europe lived to be over 80 years old!) They hide during the day and come out at night to feed on insects, crayfish and snails.

Every fall, some adult eels head back to the sea. They seem to know exactly how to get there and don't let anything get in their way. In rainy weather, eels can even travel over land. They sometimes join together into a slippery, wriggling ball and roll to the nearest body of water! Creepy — but amazing!

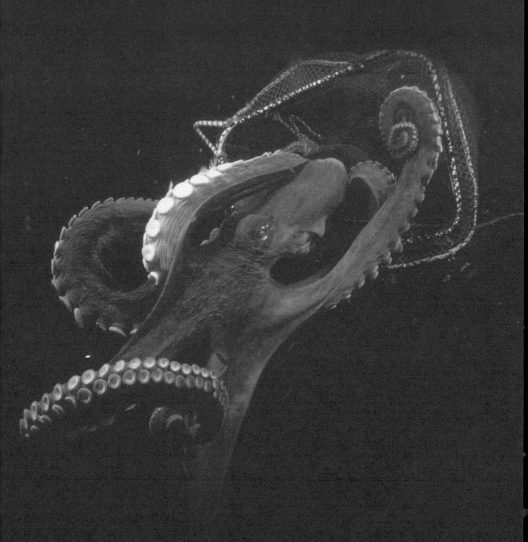

CHAPTER FOUR

Octopus

An octopus is like a superhero of the underwater world. It can disguise itself by changing colour to match what is around it. If that doesn't work, it can confuse its enemy by squirting a cloud of dark ink and then darting away!

An octopus has no bones, so it can also change its shape easily. An adult octopus can squeeze its whole body through a hole the size of its eye!

An octopus belongs to a group of animals called *cephalopods* (SE-fa-lo-pods), which means "head foot." That's because the octopus's head is attached directly to its feet, or tentacles, with nothing in between.

With so much room for brains, you might expect an octopus to be a clever creature. And you'd be right! An octopus can quickly learn how to get through a maze. It can even unscrew a jar to get at the food inside!

An octopus has another amazing trick: rocket power. To move, it takes in water and then blows it out hard. The water goes one way, and the octopus shoots off in the other direction — just like an underwater rocket!

An octopus has not one, not two, but three hearts! Two of the hearts pump blood through its gills. The other heart pumps blood to the rest of its body. And an octopus's blood is blue, not red!

Octopuses are found in all oceans of the world. The largest kind is the giant Pacific octopus. It can grow up to 7.5 metres long, from limb tip to limb tip. That would make it almost as long as a two-storey house is tall!

This giant creature starts out as a tiny egg. The female octopus lays thousands of eggs in a rocky crevice. She hangs them from the walls and keeps them clean by spraying water over them. When the eggs hatch, the octopuses are still so small that most get eaten by passing fish. But the few that survive will grow and grow . . . until they are much larger than the fish!

CHAPTER FIVE

Atlantic Puffin

A puffin is sometimes called
a sea parrot because it
is so brightly coloured.
In summer, the puffin's
multicoloured beak, face
and bright orange feet
make it easy to spot.

In winter, a puffin is not so showy.
The beak loses its colour, and the area
around its eyes turns dark. The feathers
on its head and neck thin out. A winter
puffin looks so different from
a summer puffin
that people once
thought they
were two
different birds!

Puffins have wings, but they are not the best fliers. Their short stubby wings and round bodies make it hard for them to take off. They have to flap their wings as fast as they can to stay in the air. And when they land, they often tumble head over heels, knocking over other puffins in their path!

But on the water, puffins are much more at ease. Those same short stubby wings are well suited for swimming. Their stocky bodies are just the right shape for moving quickly through the water. Their feet and legs help them steer.

Puffins need to be good swimmers because they live alone on the open sea all winter. In the spring, they come flocking back to a few special islands and shoreline cliffs along the Atlantic coast. For a few weeks, puffins can't fly because they shed their feathers and grow into their summer garb.

Then the party begins! Young males put on a show for the females. They puff out their chests, flap their wings and toss their colourful heads. When puffins find mates, they show their affection by billing: they swing their heads from side to side and tap their bills together.

Puffin couples stay together during the summer. They use their beaks and claws to dig burrows in grassy hillsides, or they use old burrows. In colder regions, where the ground is frozen, they may nest in cracks along cliff walls or in rock piles.

The female lays one egg in the nest. Both parents help keep it warm for about 40 days. When it hatches, they sit beside it and wrap a wing around it. The baby puffin, or puffling, is a cute, grey-to-black ball of fuzz!

The puffling stays in the nest for another 40 to 80 days. Its parents take turns bringing it food and keeping it safe from predators. As the puffling grows, its fuzzy coat is replaced with feathers like its parents'.

Then, one night, the puffling leaves the nest and bravely flies out over the ocean on its first solo flight. Like its parents, the young puffin spends the winter at sea. But the next spring, it finds its way back to the place where it was born.

CHAPTER SIX

Great Cormorant

There are four kinds of cormorants in Canada. The largest is the great cormorant. It lives on the Atlantic coast.

Like the puffin, the cormorant is built for life by the sea. It has a long hooked beak that is useful for catching fish, and webbed feet to help it swim.

A cormorant's feathers are specially made to let air out and water in. That means it can dive quickly and easily under the water. It also means the feathers get weighed down with water. So when the cormorant floats on the surface, only its head sticks out.

Cormorants often perch on trees or rocks with their wings spread out to dry before they take to the air.

Cormorants like to nest together in groups. They prefer steep rocky cliffs and offshore islands. Their neighbourhoods may not look very inviting, but these hard-to-reach places keep them safe from land predators.

Cormorants build their nests out of sticks. A mother and father line their nest with seaweed, grass and other materials. Then they take turns looking after the eggs. Instead of sitting on them, each bird places the eggs on its large webbed feet and covers them with its belly.

When the eggs hatch, the family stays together for another two or three months until the young birds are ready to head off on their own.

CHAPTER SEVEN

Sea Otter

A sea otter does just about everything in
the water. It eats, hunts and grooms,
all without setting foot on land. It even
sleeps on the water. A sea otter's favourite
position is floating on its back with its
paws crossed and its chin on its chest!

Of course, living this way requires some
special equipment. For one thing, an otter
has special kidneys that allow it to drink
salty sea water.

A sea otter can stay underwater for more than two minutes. It needs to stay down long enough to catch food.

An otter's fur is very important to its life in the water. An otter has little fat, so it relies on its fur to keep it warm. The fur is so thick and waterproof that an otter's skin never gets wet!

Given how important its fur is, it is not surprising that a sea otter spends a lot of time grooming. It constantly licks its coat to keep it clean. It also blows into the fur. This keeps a layer of air between its skin and the cold water.

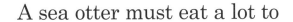

A sea otter must eat a lot to keep warm. It can devour up to 15 kilograms of food a day! It eats clams, mussels, snails, crabs and other sea creatures. To find food, an otter feels along the sea floor with its front paws. Then it brings its catch to the surface, lies on its back and uses its belly as a table!

Besides humans, very few animals use tools. The otter is one of them. It often uses a stone to crack open the hard shell of a clam or crab.

Otters are social creatures. They live in groups called rafts. Members of the raft sometimes hold each other's paws to stay close. Young otters can be found at the outer edges of the raft. Closer to the centre are the breeding males. And at the very centre are the females and their pups.

A baby otter is born in the water but can't swim for the first few weeks. Its special coat of soft fur acts like a life preserver, keeping it afloat. The mother keeps her pup on her belly most of the time. She takes good care of her pup until it is ready to look after itself.

CHAPTER EIGHT

Sea Lion

Canada's west coast is
home to two kinds
of sea lions.
The Steller's sea
lion is very large
and has a mane
of coarse hairs
around its head.

The California sea
lion is smaller
and does not
have a mane.
It is very
playful
and easy
to train.

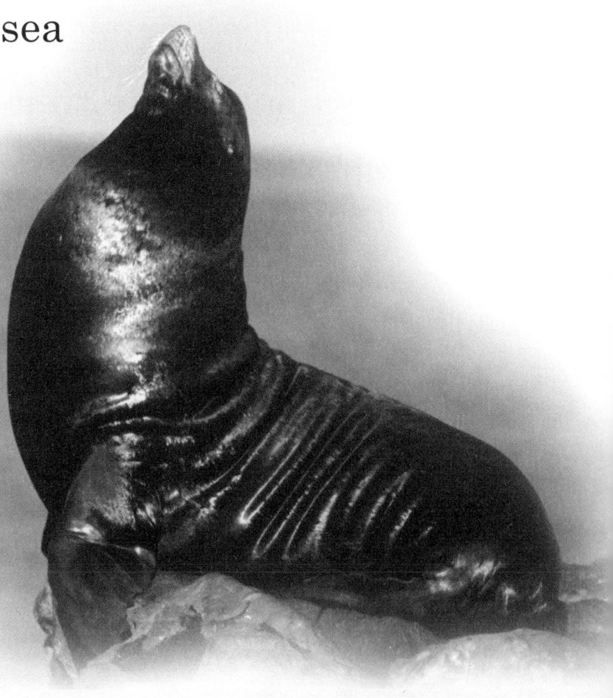

Both types of sea lions look a lot like their seal cousins. Luckily, you can tell them apart by just looking at their ears. Only sea lions have ear flaps on either side of their heads.

Another difference is how they move on land. Sea lions can use their flippers to pull themselves along. Seals have to wriggle and flop to get around!

Sea lions are very social. Often you can find them together in large groups.
And boy, are they noisy! They bark, roar, trumpet and generally make quite a racket.

In summer, the largest males gather up to 15 females and their pups to form a large "family." They roar to warn other males to stay away. Each male is often so busy protecting his family that he may not eat for up to two months. By the end of the summer, the poor male is exhausted!

Even with all the noise,
a sea lion pup can
recognize its
mother's voice.
That's a good
thing because a
pup relies on its
mother to feed
and protect it.
For the first few
weeks of life,
a baby sea lion
can't even swim.

Once they are old
enough, sea lions love the water. They can
hold their breath for up to 40 minutes.
They can also dive 180 metres beneath the
surface. That's almost the length of two
football fields end to end!

Deep under the water it is very dark.
So a sea lion relies on feel more than sight
to help it find fish, squid, crab, octopus
and clams. When a snack swims by,
the sea lion's flexible whiskers feel the
ripples in the water.

Strangely, sea lions often swallow rocks,
too. No one knows why they do this.
Do the rocks help them dive more quickly?
Or do the sea lions just mistake them for
food? What do you think?

CHAPTER NINE

Dall's Porpoise

What's black and white and swims all over? In the North Pacific Ocean, it could be a Dall's porpoise. It has a thick black body and white markings.

Dall's porpoises are the largest and fastest porpoises in the world. Porpoises often swim beside and around boats. You can tell Dall's porpoises by the spray of water they throw up: it looks like a rooster tail. These porpoises also like to zigzag back and forth so quickly that it's hard to keep track of them.

Porpoises are very smart. They talk to each other using high-pitched whistling sounds. The sounds are so high, human ears can't hear them.

Porpoises don't use their eyes to find their way around as much as we do. Instead, they use sound. Porpoises make clicking noises. The sounds travel through the water and bounce off hard objects, sending back echoes. By picking up the echoes, porpoises can tell the distance and shape of objects. This is called *echolocation* (e-ko-lo-KAY-shun).

Porpoises like to travel in groups, called pods. Most of the time, there are between 10 and 20 porpoises in a pod. Sometimes up to 200 porpoises gather in the same place to feed. It causes quite a traffic jam!

The only time a porpoise goes off on its own is to give birth. A female porpoise carries her young inside of her for a whole year. After the baby is born, the mother nurses it for two years. At first, mother and child stay apart from the rest of the pod.

Porpoises aren't fish. They are mammals and must breathe air like we do. But porpoises can hold their breath for a lot longer than we can. And they can dive much deeper to find squid, sardines, herring and other small fish to eat.

When a porpoise does surface, it takes a big breath — but not through its mouth. A porpoise breathes through a blowhole on top of its head. It has to *remember* to take in air. Otherwise, the blowhole will stay shut!

CHAPTER TEN

Humpback Whale

Humpbacks are whales, so you know they must be big. How big? Well, just the heart of a humpback weighs as much as three full-grown humans. That's big!

But their size doesn't stop them from being great acrobats. Humpbacks often leap out of the water, twirl in mid-air and SLAP the surface hard as they fall. Sometimes they stick their heads straight out of the water for a long look around. This is called spy-hopping. A humpback will also swim on its side, with its flippers in the air. Then it might slap the water hard with its tail or a flipper. We aren't exactly sure what these behaviours mean, but the whale looks like it's having fun!

A baby humpback, or calf, is born in winter when the whales are in warm southern waters. Usually, a mother, called a cow, gives birth to a single calf every one to three years. A baby humpback can drink almost 600 litres of its mother's milk a day!

A cow and her calf have a very close bond. They stay together for at least a year, and sometimes longer. Even after the calf is grown up, cow and calf are sometimes seen feeding together.

Humpbacks eat small fish and tiny swimming creatures called krill. A single whale can eat more than 2000 kilograms of food in a single day. That's a lot of krill!

That's why humpbacks have developed some clever ways to catch fish — such as bubble-net fishing. A group of whales gather under a school of fish. The whales swim in a circle, blowing upward. The fish are herded inside the wall of bubbles and are forced up toward the surface. All the whales have to do then is swim upward with their mouths wide open!

Humpback whales are best known for their singing. When they are in southern waters, they sing long, eerie songs that can be heard for hundreds of kilometres under water.

No one is sure what whalesong is for. Since only the males seem to sing, it could be a mating call. What we do know is that whales who live in the same area sing a similar song. Atlantic humpbacks sing a different song from Pacific humpbacks. Whatever the reason, whalesong is lovely to listen to — even if you are not a whale!

Swimming . . .

flying . . .

floating . . .

diving . . .

The animals along our coasts know how to live in the world around them. Some of them move easily between wet and dry, warm and cold, salty and fresh.

Canada's coastal animals are remarkable!